P9-DEU-415

THE TERRA COTTA ARMY
OF EMPEROR QIN

Caroline Lazo

A TIMESTOP BOOK

NEW DISCOVERY BOOKS
New York

Maxwell Macmillan Canada
Toronto

Maxwell Macmillan International
New York   Oxford   Singapore   Sydney

Photographic Acknowledgments
Special thanks to Dr. Robert Jacobsen and Willard L. Powell for the use of photographs from their collections.

The photo on page 76 is courtesy of AP—Wide World Photos.

New Discovery Books
Macmillan Publishing Company
866 Third Avenue
New York, NY 10022

Maxwell Macmillan Canada, Inc.
1200 Eglinton Avenue East
Suite 200
Don Mills, Ontario M3C 3N1

Macmillan Publishing Company is part of the Maxwell Communication Group of Companies.

Produced by Flying Fish Studio

Printed in the United States of America

First edition

10 9 8 7 6 5 4 3 2 1

Library of Congress Cataloging-in-Publication Data
Lazo, Caroline Evenson
    The terra cotta army of Emperor Qin / Caroline Lazo. — 1st ed.
        p. cm.
    "A timestop book."
    Includes index.
    Summary: Describes the discovery of the great clay army buried near China's Emperor Qin's tomb.
        ISBN 0-02-754631-4
    1. Qin Shih-huang, Emperor of China, 259-210 B.C.—Tomb. 2. Terra-cotta sculpture, Chinese—Qin-Han dynasties, 221 B.C. 220 A.D. 3. Shensi Province (China)—Antiquities. I.Title.
DS747.C47L39   1993
931'.04'092—dc20
    [B]   92-26189

To Stephanie, Peter, and Chip

CONTENTS

Foreword 7

Introduction 9

The Discovery 13

The Tiger of China 19

Part Man, Part Monster 24

Qin's Army Marches Again 30

A Closer Look 39

The Emperor's Weapons 50

Down-to-Earth Art 53

The Mysterious Tomb 59

Palaces and Precious Stones 61

The Miracle Workers 64

Mirror of the Ancient World 71

For Further Reading 78

Index 79

FOREWORD

Colossal might be the best word to describe the achievements of Qin Shihuangdi (259-210 B.C.), the First Emperor of China. Until he came to power in 246 B.C., China was a disorganized collection of warring states. Qin's authoritarian Legalist philosophy brought unity and peace to his country, but forced a backbreaking work schedule on the Chinese people. Through their perseverance the 2,000-mile Great Wall of China was built, and, until recently, the Wall has been the most visible reminder of the power of the First Emperor and the strength and skill of his workers.

One of the terra cotta warriors

But in 1974 we learned that the Emperor's most amazing and artistic achievement had been buried with him for more than 2,200 years. The discovery of the Emperor's tomb site—and the magnitude of the find—still stuns the world.

Chinese archaeologists continue to excavate the site surrounding the tomb at Mount Li, near Xian in Shaanxi Province, where an estimated 7,500 life-size clay figures—warriors, guards, horses, and chariots—stand 20 feet below ground. My visits to the site, and to the Museum of Warrior and Horse Figures from the Tomb of Qin Shihuangdi, Xian, never fail to remind me of the extraordinary energy and genius of the Chinese people —and of the remarkable organizational talent of Emperor Qin.

Dr. Robert Jacobsen
Curator of Asian Art
The Minneapolis Institute of Arts

*An artist's
view of
Emperor
Qin*

INTRODUCTION

Ying Zheng was only 13 years old when he became King of Qin, the largest of the warring states in ancient China. (Qin is pronounced *Chin*, and is the origin of the word *China*.) As soon as he was crowned, the young king made plans for the construction of his tomb, because he knew it would take a lifetime to build. After he unified China in 221 B.C. and proclaimed himself First Emperor, full-scale work began on the immense tomb complex, which scholars now call "one of the most extraordinary memorials on earth" and "the greatest archaeological find of our time."

Details of the tomb's scale and contents had been described in ancient folktales too bizarre for modern scholars to believe. In the *Shiji* (ancient historical records), facts about the First Emperor's tomb come to life:

> More than 700,000 workers from all parts of China laboured there. They dug through three underground streams; they poured molten copper for the outer coffin; and they filled the burial chamber with models of palaces, towers and official buildings, as well as fine utensils, precious stones and rarities. Artisans were ordered to fix automatic crossbows so that grave robbers would be slain. The waterways of the empire, the Yellow and Yang-tzu rivers . . . were represented by mercury and were made to flow mechanically. Above, the heavenly constellations were depicted. . . . An official suggested that the artisans responsible for the mechanical devices knew too much about the contents of the tomb for safety. Therefore, once the First Emperor was placed in the burial chamber and the treasures sealed up, the middle and outer gates were shut to imprison all those who had worked on the tomb. No one came out. Trees and grass were then planted over the mausoleum to make it look like a hill.

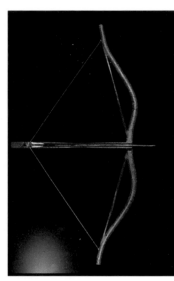

One of the crossbows placed in Qin's tomb site to prevent thieves from stealing the treasures

Rivers of mercury flowing underground? Models of palaces, towers, and buildings encased below the earth? Could such tales be true? For centuries the stories spread throughout China and aroused people's interest. But no matter how curious they were, the Chinese wouldn't dream of disturbing a tomb; such an act would have been a sacrilege and a crime. But opinions changed, and by the

20th century, the government viewed certain burial places as vivid examples of China's heritage and as valuable tools in the education of its people.

Also, modern land development began to threaten sacred sites camouflaged for centuries by grass and trees. Sometimes archaeologists have had to work fast to beat developers to the sites, not because they are opposed to new building, but because they are dedicated to preserving the beauty as well as the lessons of China's past.

No one would have guessed that a simple accident in a wheat field would lead to the discovery of the most elaborate tomb site of all. But it did.

Qin's tomb site was discovered when farmers uncovered a head like this one.

THE DISCOVERY

In March 1974 farmers digging a well in a field near the city of Xian in central China were surprised when their shovels struck a hard object 14 feet underground. They guessed it was a pottery vessel of some kind, because the tip of it was the reddish brown color of clay. But they were even more surprised when, trying to free it from the earth, they found a perfectly sculpted head of a soldier instead! Digging deeper, a life-size figure—over six feet tall—began to appear.

The farmers reported their unique find, and soon archaeologists came to the scene and continued to dig. One after another, clay figures emerged from the earth, still standing in formation 20 feet below the ground.

The location of the discovery—in a remote farmland—at once puzzled and excited scholars. "It was a time of wild anticipation," said Robert Jacobsen, Asian Art Curator at the Minneapolis Institute of Arts, "because no one knew the dimensions of the find." Questions haunted historians: Were the clay figures just an isolated, small group? Or were they part of a larger unit? If so, why were they placed in such a distant field? The nearest known ancient site—the tomb of the First Emperor—was three-quarters of a mile away, so they couldn't be a part of that site. Or could they?

Further excavation confirmed what no one had dared to imagine: The farmers had accidentally uncovered the legendary army assigned to guard the First Emperor in the afterlife, just as the ancient folktales had described.

"The remarkable quality of the statues stunned us all," said Jacobsen, a member of the first group of Americans invited to Xian, "and the size of the site—comparable in area to Cambridge, England—still boggles the mind." As more and more warriors emerged from the ground, it became clear that the mound where the tomb itself was located was just the tip of the iceberg, and that the tomb's contents could someday rival those of the tomb of Egypt's King Tutankhamen. But it will be many years before archaeologists reach the actual tomb, because thousands of clay soldiers—whole formations—must be repaired and restored along the way.

Like religious pilgrims flocking to Mecca, art historians from all over the world continue to travel to Xian to witness the unfolding of this historic discovery, which unlocks the doors to China's history of more than 2,000 years ago. They are amazed by the achievements in both art and engineering displayed in the emperor's terra cotta army. They are most impressed by the realism of the figures. Each face was individually sculpted, perhaps to look like an actual soldier in the emperor's real army. And their weapons—real weapons—are as sharp today as they were when they were buried 22 centuries ago. Though many weapons were stolen in the peasant revolt of 206 B.C. (the first peasant uprising in Chinese history), hundreds more are still in place and intact.

The warriors and their weapons leave no doubt about the First Emperor's reputation as a military genius. But historian Arthur Cotterell believes his triumph was not

Ranks of soldiers, some headless, emerge from the earth as excavation continues at the tomb site.

Visitors to the tomb site look out over an army of terra cotta warriors.

16

simply a matter of military brilliance "sweeping away" feudal states in disarray. "It was the First Emperor's role," he said, "to be China's first unifier."

The more one knows about the life of the First Emperor, the easier it is to solve the mystery of his terra cotta soldiers. Seeing them only in the sunlight of the 20th century is like walking in at the end of a great movie; without knowing what has gone before, the ending makes little sense.

Who Was the First Emperor?

Between 230 and 221 B.C., King Ying Zheng conquered all of his neighboring feudal states and befriended the outlying ones. In this way the country of China was born. To honor this great achievement, the young king proclaimed himself Qin Shihuangdi, the First Emperor. Shihuangdi (pronounced Shee-wang-dee) combines three words: shi, meaning first, and huang and di, meaning kings of the past.

By taking the title First Emperor, Qin confirmed his superiority over the neighboring kings and achieved divinity in the eyes of his people. "Let me be called Sovereign Emperor," he proclaimed. But his harsh, authoritarian rule, combined with his mighty feats, earned him another title, Tiger of China.

Qin was also likened to the dragon, a highly regarded deity in Chinese mythology. The dragon was lord of the waters, the rainmaker, and his powers were magical. According to myth, "He could soar through clouds and also penetrate the deepest springs." The First Emperor chose water as the imperial symbol because water puts out fire, and fire symbolized the previous Xhou dynasty. Qin believed in the power of the five elements (fire, water, earth, wood, and metal), and his reign became known as the Power of Water.

Qin selected black for the color of his court—robes, banners, and flags—and called his people "the blackhaired ones." He used the number six as the standard measurement; a soldier's pace was six feet, carriages were six feet wide, and the imperial carriage had six horses. Laws dealing with these details were strict, as ancient records noted: "The law was harsh and there were no amnesties."

The dragon, a central figure in Chinese mythology, came to represent Emperor Qin.

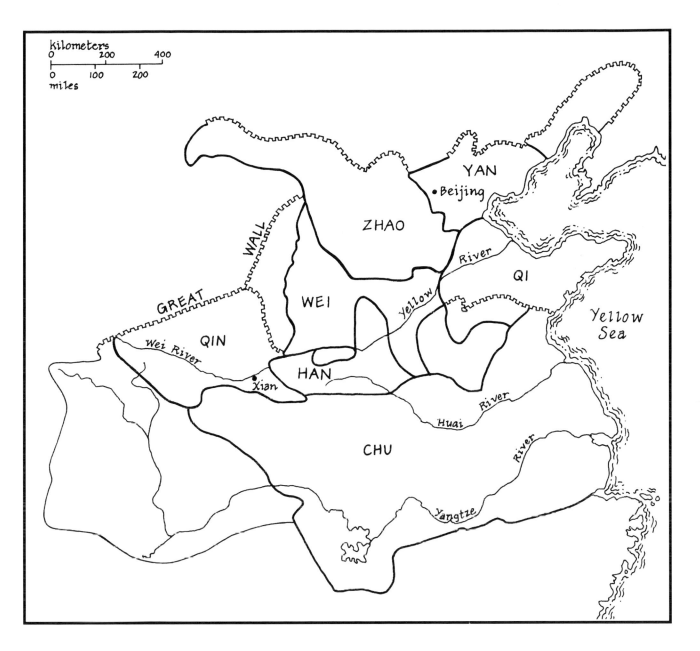

THE TIGER OF CHINA

Even as a young boy Qin dreamed of ending the constant fighting among the seven states—Qi, Yan, Zhao, Han, Wei, Chi, and Qin—and of bringing peace to China. But not until he became king of the largest state could he harness enough power and form a strategy to end the Warring States period, which had begun 254 years earlier.

To Qin, a country made up of unfriendly, separate states, each one with its own laws, language, and form of writing, was really no country at all. But once united, the states would be strong and secure, he believed, and more successful in defending themselves against foreign invaders. Though he was convinced he was right, he knew the longtime rulers of the other states would challenge him. After all, if their borders dissolved, so would their power.

Consultation with other kings was not Qin's style. He was a visionary with the creation of a country on his mind, and nothing could distract him from his goal. He wanted to do it his way, with force, because war was the language everyone understood. Like a tiger on the prowl, he would stake out his territory, plot his moves, and ready his army for attack.

Qin used the art of deception to systematically defeat the states. According to the *Shiji*, he swallowed them up "as a silkworm devours a mulberry leaf." Give the enemy reason to relax, Qin said, then strike with all your might "with a million strong and a thousand chariots." Then, like a tiger, Qin went in for the kill: "Engage an enemy and be sure to vanquish it, storm a city and take it without fail, make a clean sweep of all that dare to stand in the way."

But unification demanded more than the breakdown of borders. Language barriers and currency differences had to be removed, too. Qin standardized weights and measures, and he developed a uniform system of writing. In doing so, he brought the people closer together and generated trade throughout China. His most celebrated projects, however, tested the skills and stamina of the people forced to build them.

Qin relied on the peasantry for his empire's growth in both peace and war; about 15 percent of the total population of 20 million worked on his projects. They constructed a network of roads that even the Romans would have envied. They built a palace larger than any in the world—three times the size of the great throne hall in China's capital, Beijing, and eight times the size of the White House in Washington, D.C. To protect the country from intruders, Qin drafted 500,000 workers to build the 2,000-mile Great Wall—the only human-made structure visible from outer space by astronauts.

One of Qin's greatest achievements, the Great Wall winds across the Chinese landscape.

While his achievements dazzled the world, their cost to his country was high. Agriculture suffered because of the dearth of workers; those who were diverted to public works endured great hardships—heavy taxes, long hours of service, and cruel punishment for small mistakes. Fear of rebellion plagued the First Emperor. Even as a young king, thoughts of death obsessed him and spawned his lifelong search for immortality.

Assassination plots early in Qin's reign increased his fear of death, his distrust of those around him, and his doubts about everyone else. He tightened his close circle of advisers as well as the reins of power. To insure law and order, capital punishment became common in China. He even placed his mother under house arrest! When Confucian scholars publicly defended traditional family authority and denounced Qin's one-man rule, Li Su, Qin's chief adviser, launched the Burning of the Books in 213 B.C. Li Su proclaimed: "These scholars learn only from the old, not from the new, and employ their learning to oppose our rule. . . . Let all historical records but those of the First Emperor be destroyed."

Those "historical records" included manuscripts of music, and historians believe that *The Classic of Music* by Confucius, one of the most important works of its kind, was among those burned. All books were destroyed except those dealing with Qin's favorite topics—mainly medicine, agriculture, and supernatural events.

When China became unified in 221 B.C., Li Su became Qin's grand councillor. He managed the emperor's building programs and promoted his philosophy of legalism (rule by strict laws) throughout all 36 prefectures (official districts) of the country. Without strict laws and a supreme power in charge, China would fall apart, Qin claimed. He believed that people were evil by nature and that only laws could control their behavior. Qin based his philosophy on the teachings of Shang Yang and Han Feizi, who convinced him that the promise of severe punishment would deter people from opposing him. Han Feizi wrote: "If the laws are weak, so is the kingdom. . . . The ruler alone should possess the power, wielding it like lightning or thunder."

And wield it like lightning and thunder Qin did. In 212 B.C., one year after the Burning of the Books, Qin ordered the execution of 460 scholars suspected of opposing him by thwarting his search for eternal life. Only one of his own children (he had more than 20, whose mothers are unknown) dared to challenge the emperor's order—and he was sentenced to death along with the scholars.

The massacre of the scholars would never be forgotten in Chinese history. It not only inspired the people's revolt in 206 B.C., but would come back to haunt the country 2,000 years later.

While the Great Wall kept China's enemies out, it also kept Qin's people in.

PART MAN, PART MONSTER

Unlike other rulers in China, Qin rose to power through the shrewd planning of his father, a wealthy merchant, and not through the usual ancestral ties. And Qin selected his ministers and military officers because of their abilities, not because of their old family connections. He was the first ruler in Chinese history to do so.

He was China's first practical ruler. The Great Wall, for example, was not built to honor his ancestors or to please the gods; it was built to keep foreign intruders out and his own people in. All of his programs—new roads, currency, uniform laws—were designed to build communication among the people and bring peace and prosperity to China. An ancient inscription sums up Qin's accomplishments:

Great are the Sovereign's achievements . . .
All men under Heaven
Toil with a common purpose.
Tools and measures are the same,
The written script is standardized . . .
Wherever the sun and moon shine
Wherever one can go by boat or by carriage
Men obey their orders
And satisfy their desires.
For our Sovereign in accordance with the time
Has regulated local customs,
Constructed waterways and divided up the land . . .
He works day and night without rest
He defines the laws leaving none in doubt,
Making known what is forbidden . . .
Administration is smoothly carried out
All is done correctly, all according to plan . . .
No evil or impropriety is tolerated,
So all strive to be excellent men
And exert themselves in tasks great and small.
The ordinary people know peace,
Having laid aside weapons and armour . . .
There are no robbers or thieves . . .
All things flourish and grow.

But writer Jia Yi (201-169 B.C.) saw things differently, as expressed in his famous essay, "The Sins of Qin":

He climbed to the highest position and extended his sway over the six directions, scourging the world with his rod, and shaking the four seas with his power . . . Then, he discarded the ways of the former kings and burned the writings of the Hundred Schools in order to keep his people mired in ignorance. He tore down the great fortifications of the states, executed their powerful leaders, collected all the arms of the Empire . . . all this in order to weaken the people.

Qin's strong personality, especially his determination to prove that he was greater than all other rulers, was the driving force behind China's growth. As historian Arthur Cotterell pointed out, however, the First Emperor's "outbursts of fury" showed how insensitive he could be: "When he found crossing the Yangtze river difficult because of a gale," Cotterell wrote, "the First Emperor placed blame on the river-goddess whose temple stood on a mountain close by. In retaliation he ordered 3,000 convicts to fell all the trees on its slopes, leaving the mountain bare."

Trees, Qin said, should serve a practical purpose and should not be planted for their beauty alone, as noted in the records of the time: "The planting of the green pine tree was what gave beauty to the roads. Yet . . . this was done so that the First Emperor's successors should not have to take circuitous routes." And pines were ordered for his tomb site because they possessed eternal energy and might help him achieve immortality. In ancient China many believed that sap from certain trees could prolong one's life by 500 years.

If anyone deserved immortality, Qin claimed, it was he. His efforts to contact immortals to find the elixir, or magic formula, for long life continued to the end. In Taoism, often called the Philosophy of Nature, he found new interest in supernatural powers, but the elixir still eluded him.

Historical records from 212 B.C. report that Qin ordered several hundred astrologers to watch the stars for answers. But the astrologers felt intimidated by the Emperor and were afraid of offending him, so they flattered him and kept all negative signs a secret. And no wonder! He killed the whole population of a village when he heard that some unfavorable comments about him had been carved on a meteorite that had landed there.

But why would a practical man like the First Emperor rely on magicians and astrologers for information and advice? How could such a practical person consider living forever in the first place?

Some historians believe Qin might have gone mad with power and was unable to imagine China existing without him. They think he panicked at the thought of losing influence over future generations. Others believe Qin wanted to become a god, since many of his servants already worshiped him as such and called him "the divine power." He was the first to ever use the title of Emperor, which elevated him above everyone. So, to him, the quest for immortality wasn't impractical at all; it was the only logical way he could find to fulfill his awesome title.

In the last years of his life, Qin focused all of his attention on his tomb and the details of its construction. He enlarged the work force to more than half a million laborers, surpassing the number assigned to the Great Wall. Careful preparations were made for his journey into the afterlife, including the creation of a full army to protect him and the gathering of symbols of immortality to surround him. Workers spent 30 years building the emperor's tomb complex, covering 22 square miles, and were still working on it the day he died.

Part of Qin's guardian army

Just how big this undertaking was would one day shock the world.

While touring the provinces along the Yellow Sea, Qin made one last stab at securing immortality. His chief adviser, Grand Councillor Li Su, had told him to kill a huge fish with a repeater crossbow because in doing so he would kill the evil spirit that kept him from contacting the immortals. And so he did.

After he killed the fish (probably a whale), Emperor Qin became ill, and died a few days later. Li Su feared for his life, so he kept the news of Qin's death quiet and ordered the heir apparent, Prince Fu-su, to commit suicide to prevent him from taking over as emperor. He then faked a will appointing Qin's second son, Hu-hai (the more favorable to Li Su) as his successor. The imperial entourage then proceeded to the palace, greeting people along the way as if nothing had happened. The *Shiji* describes that final ride:

> The coffin was borne in a litter [an enclosed, curtained, canopylike bed with shafts for carrying] escorted by attendants who presented food and official reports as usual and issued imperial commands from the covered litter. . . . But it was summer and the litter began to smell. To disguise the stench the escort was told to load a cart with salted fish.

So the great unifier of China and ruler of "all under Heaven" rode home that day in 210 B.C. covered in silks but reeking of fish.

Qin's son Hu-hai became the second sovereign emperor, and nine months later, Qin, the Tiger of China, was buried at Mount Li.

Three years after the Emperor's death, the peasants finally rose up against his harsh laws and brought an end to his empire. They broke into Qin's tomb and burned and looted some of its contents. The guards' crossbows, which had been positioned to spring into action automatically if anyone tried to enter the tomb, apparently failed to find their marks.

The secret of the emperor's tomb site remained safe for more than 2,000 years—until the day in March 1974 when farmers accidentally struck the head of a life-size clay soldier standing 20 feet below the ground. This was just the tip of the iceberg. By 1990 Chinese archaeologists had found and restored hundreds of clay soldiers, as well as horses, chariots, and real weapons.

Today a unique arched building called the Museum of Warrior and Horse Figures from the Tomb of Qin Shihuangdi protects the terra cotta army. "Without any question," says Dr. Jacobsen, "this is the most exciting archaeological find of our time . . . and the burial chamber hasn't even been reached yet!"

The Museum of Warrior and Horse Figures from the Tomb of Qin Shihuangdi

Once a closely guarded secret, the tomb site of Emperor Qin is now open to the public.

QIN'S ARMY MARCHES AGAIN

The location of the First Emperor's tomb, between Mount Li and the Wei River, was chosen because of the ancient Taoist belief that the land between wind and water was free of evil spirits. But the sacred pines and cypresses that once covered the hill have long since disappeared, and the Great Sovereign Emperor now rests beneath an ordinary apricot orchard. "They are probably the most precious apricots in the world!" Dr. Jacobsen says.

Though the first discovery of the tomb site was made in 1974, several years passed before Chinese leaders fully lifted the ban on foreign travel into their country and gave outsiders a look at the historic find. At first the government permitted only selected visitors—scientists, political leaders, and art historians—to view the remarkable treasures buried there for 22 centuries. Meanwhile, newspaper headlines around the world announced the event: THE FIRST EMPEROR'S ARMY MARCHES AGAIN; ANCIENT TOMB FIGURES EMERGE FROM CHINA'S SOIL; and FARMERS FIND FIRST EMPEROR'S SECRET ARMY.

By 1981 tourists were allowed to travel to Xian, the capital of Shaanxi Province, and reporter Sherry Ricchiardi of the *Des Moines Register* described her visit there:

> We were loaded onto a rickety bus and taken for a painfully slow ride through a countryside dotted with wheat fields. . . . Finally, our guide motioned us toward a huge Quonset hut-like structure. Suddenly, in dusty, dimly lit surroundings, the forbidden became real. Even an elderly couple who three times had circled the globe wiped tears from their eyes. The ruin of 2,200 years failed to dull the spectacle of the underground battlefield, with rows of helmeted warriors standing side by side. . . . Some glared fiercely, others appeared on the verge of a smile.

Excavation continues at the tomb site, parts of which may remain buried for years to come.

Plan of Pit No. 1

•••• Armored and unarmored soldiers

Six chariots at east end

So far, four pits have been discovered at Mount Li. The largest of these, Pit No. 1, covers an area of almost four acres. It contains nearly 6,000 terra cotta soldiers, bowmen, crossbowmen, archers, and six horse-drawn chariots with charioteers. Terra cotta, meaning "baked earth" (or clay), was used for the figures, because the coarse clay found in the area was heavy enough to form life-size sculptures. Once formed, the figures were fired (baked hard) in large, brick kilns (ovens) at high temperatures. The source of fire was wood—also plentiful in surrounding areas.

Still in formation, Qin's warriors have stood at attention for more than 2,000 years.

*Poised for attack,
a terra cotta soldier
appears frozen in time.*

Though made of clay, the soldiers look alive and alert.
The crossbowmen in front look ready to attack, and the
infantrymen behind them appear just as brave. And no
two faces are alike. Such individuality of expression had
never been seen before in Chinese art. Are they replicas of
actual soldiers in Qin's army? Many historians believe so,
but no one is certain. Some believe they reflect the great
variety of people Qin brought together when he unified
China. Still others wonder if they might be the faces of the
workers who made them, the workers having used one
another as models.

The figures in Pit No. 1 stand in military formation, and they all face east. Though only the officers wear helmets, most of the soldiers in the infantry wear armor. Two hundred unarmored bowmen and crossbowmen form the front ranks, and eleven corridors of foot soldiers stand in tight formation behind them. Two rows of archers make up the outer two ranks and appear poised to hold off enemy attacks from either side.

Two soldiers, both wearing distinctive armor, stand at the ready.

Each soldier in Qin's terra cotta army wears his own kind of armor. This figure is an archer.

Though the clay warriors serve as guards, they do not carry shields. Qin's soldiers never used shields because he claimed that alertness and bravery were the most reliable forms of protection in battle. Nor did their armor fully cover them, which made them more agile than the enemy in the field. (The nobility who rode in the chariots, however, were protected by lacquered shields.)

*A command
chariot from
Qin's tomb site*

The charioteers are equipped with more armor than all the rest of the soldiers. Each of their suits consists of 324 separate plates. (Qin's real soldiers wore suits made of lacquered leather, it is believed, because similar metal plates have not been found.)

The six horse-drawn wooden chariots follow close behind the unarmored infantry, and three rows of armored infantry stand ready to protect the rear. Two of the chariots carry drums and bells, which commanding officers used when giving orders to their troops in battle. And their orders were not meant to be taken lightly, as Sun Zi noted in *The Art of War*:

"Now gongs and drums, banners and flags are used to focus the attention of the troops. When the troops can thus be united, the brave cannot advance alone, nor can the cowardly withdraw. So it follows that those who [disobey] are beheaded."

Armor: The Qin Style

Before the discovery of the terra cotta soldiers, we knew little about the armor worn in Qin's time. The first armor used in China dates back to the Shang dynasty (1765-1027 B.C.), and it was made of painted leather strips. Much later, in the Warring States period, soldiers wore lacquered leather plates laced together with fine leather thongs.

Judging by the clay army, Qin's soldiers wore eight different styles of armor, including some that slipped on over the head, some that fit like a vest, and some with neck guards and sleeves. A common style resembles a baseball catcher's protective vest supported by straps crisscrossed in back. More elaborate armor was reserved for commanding officers.

The terra cotta armor worn by Qin's soldiers matches the armor worn by real soldiers from that period.

Depending on one's rank and function in the emperor's army, armor could be very simple or extremely intricate. Since Qin's troops were known for their "untold ferocity" and swiftness on the battlefield, they needed great flexibility as well as protection in their armor. The light clothing worn by the crossbowmen indicates for the first time the importance Qin placed on offensive power. It is likely that he had the largest, best-equipped, and most professional army in the world at that time.

A kneeling soldier

Each of the 7,500 members of the terra cotta army has individual facial expressions.

A CLOSER LOOK

Though the faces of the clay figures are individualized, their torsos are similar. From the waist down the statues are solid; the upper parts are hollow. Each figure is indeed the sum of its parts. The body was made first, followed by the head, arms, hands, and facial details. When first uncovered, the figures appeared to have been made from molds because there were so many of them. But on close examination it became clear that the faces and details of every soldier were finished by hand.

This drawing shows what Qin's army might have looked like when first painted.

After completing the statues, workers painted them with colorful vegetable dyes, which over time have dissolved or flaked off. But a few traces of paint still remain and provide clues to the original bright colors. A general, for example, wore a black tunic over a red one, green leggings, yellow shoulder pads, and a head bonnet with red ties. A group of infantrymen had black armor plates with white rivets, gold buttons, and purple cords. Their cloaks were green with lavender collars and cuffs, and their pants were dark blue. Another group wore red tunics with light blue collars and cuffs; their armor was brown with red rivets and orange cords. The heads of the figures were painted, too, and the hair, not surprisingly, was black—recalling Emperor Qin's favorite name for his people, "the blackhaired ones."

Like the faces of the statues, the hairstyles are individualized, and so carefully detailed that every strand of hair is visible. The infantrymen wear their hair in a knot on the top of the head, slanted to the right, and display many different styles of braiding. The cavalrymen wear caps with chin straps, while officers and charioteers have stiff bonnets. Both armored and unarmored soldiers wear leggings and square-toed sandals.

Infantry men (top) and a cavalryman (bottom) from Qin's army

The height and uniform of this soldier indicate that he is an officer.

Rank is indicated by the design of a soldier's armor and headgear, the tassels on his tunic, and by his size. The foot soldiers average 5'10"; officers are 6' tall and over. The tallest figure, the lead commander in Pit No. 2, measures 6'4".

The horses, too, had a colorful past. Their coats were originally black or brown, and their ears, mouths, and nostrils were red. Their hooves and teeth were painted white. Even their saddles, made of leather and metal, were once brightly painted—red, white, brown, and blue.

A row of horses waits to lead Qin's army into battle.

Like their human counterparts, the horses of Qin's army each have individual facial expressions.

Like the soldiers, the horses' bodies are hollow and their legs solid. With heads raised high, eyes wide open, and ears pointed up, they appear alert, strong, and determined—like the warriors themselves—and ready to pull their chariots at the crack of a whip.

Whole chariots have been reconstructed from the pieces of wood and other fragments of the original war chariots found in the pits during the first excavations. One unit alone contains 64 chariots! In more recent explorations west of the tomb, two bronze four-horse chariots were uncovered in Pit No. 2, located 66 feet north of Pit No. 1. Pit No. 3 appears to be the headquarters for the terra cotta army, because the war chariot of the

Archaeologists work to restore some of the horses and chariots at the tomb site.

commander in chief was discovered there. Many of his officers were found there, too, but the commander himself hasn't been uncovered, and his whereabouts remain a mystery.

Chariots were most efficient when used in wide-open, flat areas of the country. But in Emperor Qin's time, battles were often fought on rugged and uneven terrain, so chariots became less effective than saddle horses and mounted soldiers, especially when confronting foreign intruders along mountainous borders. In Pit No. 2, however, chariot units and cavalry are almost the same in number. To some historians this means that the First Emperor still valued the chariot, particularly as a symbol of superior power. To Emperor Qin, the ideal army was "a million strong with a thousand chariots." Together, according to ancient accounts, they would "storm a city, take it without fail and make a clean sweep of all that dared to stand in the way."

Though Pit No. 3 is only about one-seventh the size of Pit No. 1, its special function as the command headquarters for the nearly 8,000-piece army fascinates art historians and military experts alike. But if the commander in chief is missing, how can they be sure it is the headquarters? In addition to his war chariot, other clues have emerged: The soldiers are stationed as guards to protect their (absent) leader; their armor is both light mail (overlapping scales of lacquered leather) to allow quick movement, and heavier mail (probably iron) used for close fighting; and some of the weapons found in Pit No. 3 are a ceremonial kind traditionally identified with a commander in chief. But until he is found, questions about his identity remain unanswered.

Plan of Pit No. 2

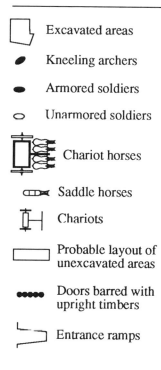

Excavated areas

Kneeling archers

Armored soldiers

Unarmored soldiers

Chariot horses

Saddle horses

Chariots

Probable layout of unexcavated areas

Doors barred with upright timbers

Entrance ramps

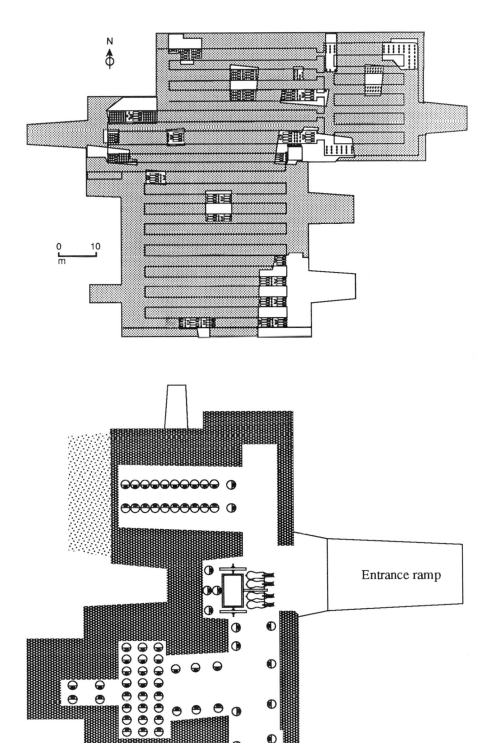

N

0   10
m

Plan of Pit No.3

Warriors

Chariot horses

Earth support

Firmly pounded earth support

Entrance ramp

Mencius: Philosopher or Prophet?

While viewing the terra cotta warriors, questions arise about the spirit of the times in which Qin amassed his incredible power. Were all voices of opposition silenced? Did the Burning of the Books and the killing of the scholars suppress all thought or hope of rebellion? Not all. The voice of Mencius, a philosopher, remained constant for generations. His teachings, many believe, inspired the peasant revolt that finally ended the Qin dynasty.

Mencius (372-289 B.C.) was a prominent disciple of Confucius, the founding father of Chinese philosophy and education. Though Mencius favored discipline and orderliness in government, he warned about the dangers of one-man rule and lack of sensitivity to the feelings and needs of the people. "Heaven sees accordingly as the people see, Heaven hears accordingly as the people hear." Those lines from an ancient poem inspired the philosopher, but they passed right over the head of the headstrong emperor.

The people, Mencius said, were the heart of the country, and only if they were healthy and happy could their ruler enjoy lasting peace. Mencius spoke out against war and urged kings to show compassion. "A benevolent man," he wrote, "extends his love from those he loves to those he does not love. A ruthless man extends his ruthlessness from those he does not love to those he loves." Kindness, he believed, was a reflection of the chun-tzu *(superior person and protector of truth), who couldn't bear to see people suffer.*

Mencius might be called the first father of democracy, a man well ahead of his time and, maybe, of our own. "Weapons," he said, "however highly decorated, are instruments of destruction. The wise man will have nothing to do with them." But in China at the time, war was a way of life. With so many borders to defend, battles were constant until Qin unified the feudal states. And to make a clean sweep of them, he saw war as his only option. So he built the strongest army in the world, an army so fearful of his punitive laws that it didn't dare lose even the smallest battle. Given the most advanced weapons of the time—both iron and bronze—victory was inevitable. But lasting peace, as Mencius predicted, was not.

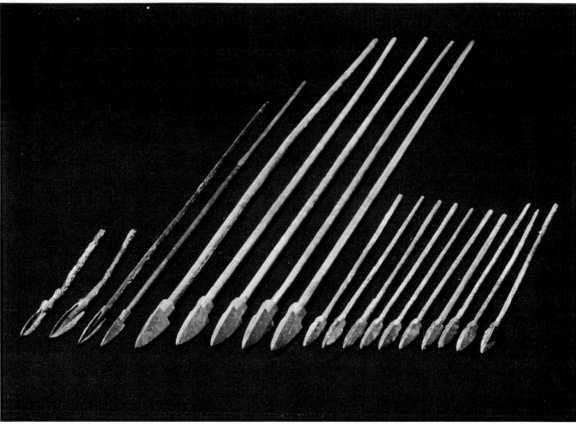

Arrows and spears found in Qin's tomb site still remain sharp after centuries underground.

THE EMPEROR'S WEAPONS

Though the tomb figures are made of clay, their weapons are real. "The bronze swords and arrowheads are as sharp today as when they were cast 2,200 years ago," writes historian Qian Hao. More than 10,000 parts of weapons have been found, including bows and crossbows for distance fighting, and spears, swords, broadswords, halberds, and other weapons for close combat. The metals used most often are copper and tin alloys, with traces of nickel, vanadium, bismuth, zinc, silicon, titanium, manganese, chromium, cobalt, and niobium. The carefully balanced amounts of raw materials used in the weapons point to the progress made in military science and technology in Qin's time.

Qin's soldiers carried double-edged swords in wooden sheaths, but they were used only by the cavalry, charioteers, and officers. The infantry carried the deadlier halberd, a daggerlike blade with a long wooden shaft. Because of the many trigger parts of crossbows found at the tomb site, that weapon appears to have been more popular during Qin's reign than ever before. Originally painted red, the crossbow was the deadliest weapon of all, able to penetrate the enemy's armor from great distances. Unlike the longbow, hand-operated by the archer, the crossbow was mechanically set.

A sword carried by one of the terra cotta warriors

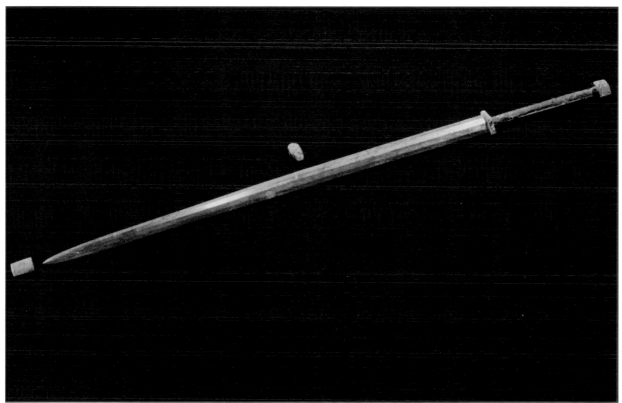

Arrow and spearheads from the tomb site

As noted earlier, Qin ordered crossbows to be set in his tomb to attack or ward off robbers. But historical records show that rebel forces plundered the pits for weapons following the downfall of the Qin dynasty. In spite of looting and damage, thousands of weapons were found intact. In Pit No. 2, for example, archaeologists discovered more than 1,400 bronze arrowheads, still sharp enough to split a hair! More weapons are expected to appear as digging progresses.

The terra cotta soldiers not only prove the military genius of the First Emperor but, more important, they provide the first examples of monumental art in China.

Because of the lifelike faces of the terra cotta warriors, some people think they were modeled after Qin's own soldiers.

DOWN-TO-EARTH ART

Emperor Qin's practical nature and clear-cut views are evident in the terra cotta tomb figures. The face of each statue is so realistically modeled that qualities of mood, age, and personal character can be seen. Some frown and some smile, as they reveal varied degrees of inner control and confidence.

Such realism in Chinese art was unheard of before Qin's time. In the Zhou period (1027-771 B.C.), for example, art most often reflected the superstitions that slave owners fostered to terrify their slaves. No wonder the *Taotie* "monster mask" and the slave in a tiger's mouth were popular images! But in the Warring States period (475-221 B.C.) activities from everyday life—hunting and fighting—and images of silkworms began to appear on bronze vessels.

Qin's clay army advanced Chinese art much further. "Even the heads of rivets on their coats of mail have been modeled," writes historian Arthur Cotterell. But it is the facial expressiveness that separates the tomb figures from the art of other cultures at the time. In ancient Greece, for example, sculptors would soften and idealize the faces of their subjects, who were usually deities or great men of the past, not contemporary soldiers or palace guards.

One of the 7,500 faces of Qin's army

The lines around the eyes, the crow's feet, the turned-up corners of the mouths, and the various mustaches enhance the realism of Qin's clay soldiers. And all ages—from young-looking recruits to stern old commanders—are represented in the terra cotta army. Their overall readiness, their alert stance, and their varied expressions leave no doubt about the insight and skills of the 700,000 Chinese people who spent 30 years building the tomb complex.

Two soldiers stand at the ready while excavation goes on around them.

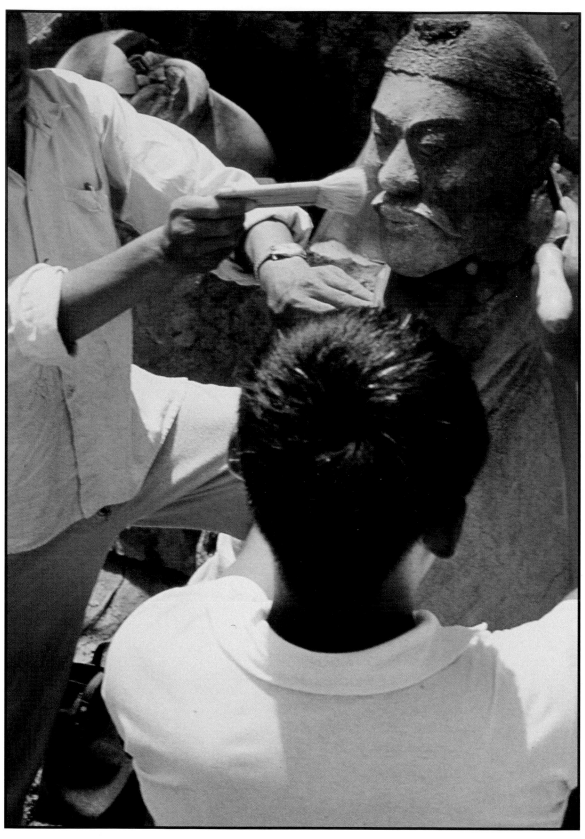

Careful excavation and restoration ensures that the terra cotta warriors look just as they did when they were first made.

A restored warrior and his horse greet visitors to the tomb site museum.

Restoration

Three of the four pits discovered so far contain the terra cotta army, horses, and chariots; the fourth is empty. An on-site museum, the Museum of Warrior and Horse Figures from the Tomb of Qin Shihuangdi, has been built over Pit No. 1. From there, visitors can see 210 soldiers standing where they were originally placed 2,200 years ago. Since only a fraction of the pit has been excavated, both excavation and repairs continue there. Today, museum buildings cover pits No. 2 and No. 3 as well.

Before restoring a figure, Chinese archaeologists and their assistants clean each broken piece of clay by hand with small brushes, and in the process they must record each step of their work and photograph every piece found. Restoration is painstaking work; the color, form, and place of discovery of every article found must be recorded before a figure can be glued together and displayed. One figure can involve hundreds of pieces! Artists assist the workers with detailed drawings of each object discovered on the way to the tomb. No wonder it will take years before archaeologists can begin to excavate the tomb itself.

"We must have patience," Dr. Jacobsen says, "because, after all, this is a sacred site involving historic treasures, and every piece found there is a valuable part of the whole. . . .It takes keen eyes and skilled hands to repair these incredible figures and position them as originally intended. That is what restoration is all about."

THE MYSTERIOUS TOMB

If the statues guarding the tomb site of Emperor Qin are any indication, the treasures still to be found will be amazing.

"They poured molten copper for the outer coffin; and they filled the burial chamber with models of palaces, towers and official buildings, as well as fine utensils, precious stones and rarities." If those words from the *Shiji* are correct, many surprises are in store when archaeologists finally open Qin's tomb. The *Shiji* is the only detailed historical record of the First Emperor's reign. Sima Qian compiled the information from folktales as well as official and private libraries, but he actually wrote the account a hundred years after the downfall of the Qin dynasty. So far, the discoveries at Mount Li have led experts to agree that Qin's tomb may be exactly as described in the ancient record. "If it escaped plundering by rebel forces," said Jacobsen, "the tomb could astonish us even more than the incredible terra cotta soldiers who guard it."

59

The tomb mound that covers the burial place of Qin

The tomb is located three-quarters of a mile east of the pits, where excavation and restoration of the terra cotta army continue. In 210 B.C. protective walls guarded the site. An inner wall measured 2,247 by 1,896 feet; the outer wall was 7,129 by 3,196 feet; and the total area covered about three-quarters of a square mile. Today, the huge mound still rises 164 feet above ground level and is 4,593 feet in circumference. Its enormous bulk was meant to symbolize the great accomplishments of Emperor Qin.

PALACES AND PRECIOUS STONES

According to the *Shiji*, Qin built 300 palaces in the Wei River area, and 400 outside of it: "Connected by elevatcd avenues and courts with pavilions, [the palaces] were filled with the beautiful women and instruments captured from the different states."

Qin had hundreds of mistresses—and built a palace for each one! In addition, he built mansions for the kings he conquered so that China's wealth could be concentrated in his capital. At the same time, he could more easily monitor the activities of the former feudal lords.

Toward the end of his life, tormented by the search for immortality, Qin increased his building program to include secret passageways connecting all of his palaces and buildings so that evil spirits couldn't find him. Galleries, gardens, and parks surrounded the palaces. The largest palace of all was called *Afang*, meaning "beside the capital," and it measured almost half a mile in length. The *Shiji* describes the ancient setting:

> Then he had palaces constructed in the Shanglin gardens, south of the Wei river. The front palace, Afang, was built first. . . .The terraces above could seat 10,000, and below there was room for banners [66 feet] in height. One causeway round the palace led to the South Hill at the top of which a gateway was erected. A second led across the Wei river to (the capital), just as the Heavenly Corridor in the sky leads from the Apex of Heaven across the Milky Way to the Royal Chamber.

Qin brought not only the vanquished kings to the capital, but their weapons, too, which "were melted into bells and bell supports, and made into twelve metal (bronze) human figures, each weighing thousands of pounds, these being set up within the imperial palace."

Though only fragments of the actual Afang's walls remain, there is reason to believe that a replica of the whole palace awaits archaeologists when they open the tomb—along with "fine utensils, precious stones and rarities." The prospect of finding a model of this palace in the Emperor's tomb excites everyone involved in the excavation at Mount Li.

One precious stone above all had special meaning in ancient China: jade. Before a body was buried, the eyes and tongue were covered with pieces of jade so that the body would stay intact and the soul would not escape. Professor R. W. L. Guisso describes the importance of this precious stone in *The First Emperor of China*:

> The Chinese believed that man possessed twin souls that parted company at death—one to lie in a tomb and the other to ascend to the heavens. Both required the sacrifice and offerings of jade . ..Kings had jade strung into girdle pendants worn over their robes to make tinkling sounds when they walked through the palace, and there are accounts of powdered jade being eaten to prolong life.

Jade symbolized wealth and power. Since no one loved power more than Qin, there is no doubt that much jade will be found in his tomb.

Even miniature rivers are expected to be found in Qin's tomb: "The waterways of the empire, the Yellow and Yang-tzu rivers, and even the great ocean itself, were represented by mercury and were made to flow mechanically." That statement from the *Shiji* may sound farfetched, but after the discovery of the clay army, the soil of the surrounding area was tested, and electronic sensors found 120 times more mercury around the tomb complex than in all the rest of the soil! "If we find rivers of mercury as well as replicas of palaces, we won't be surprised," says Dr. Jacobsen, "because to the First Emperor nothing was impossible."

The genius behind the tomb site of Emperor Qin is evident in the rows of flawless statues that guard the dead ruler's secrets.

THE MIRACLE WORKERS

After seeing the terra cotta army, visitors always ask the same question: How did he do it? Without bulldozers and other modern equipment, how could 7,500 life-size figures be modeled and assembled 20 feet below ground? How could a 2,000-mile wall and a palace eight times the size of the White House be built at the same time—not to mention 700 other palaces and networks of roads and waterways?

We know the First Emperor was a master planner, but it was his labor force that turned his dreams into realities. And it was the strongest work force in the history of ancient China.

As historian Cotterell describes, the building of the Emperor's tomb complex required both strength and ingenuity on the part of the workers:

> These subterranean chambers were skillfully built; the rammed earth surrounding the corridors and galleries prevented subsidence [sliding down], while each chamber was paved with bricks and its wooden roof was supported by stout timber pillars and crossbeams. To prevent moisture seeping down from the surface, the roof was covered by woven matting and then a layer of clay.

Jumbled together, some of the terra cotta soldiers wait to be restored.

And even before their work on the Emperor's tomb began, the laborers had to find and transport all of the building materials to the tomb site. Two thousand years ago that could have been their heaviest burden of all.

What motivated the workers to endure such hardship? Modern ideas such as "employee benefits" would never have occurred to a tyrant like Qin. He gave his workers a way to survive, and it was the only way they knew. Yet even that wasn't secure.

Many of the people who worked on Qin's tomb site were actually prisoners serving time for crimes they had committed.

Forced labor was a common punishment for breaking laws under Qin's rule. Of the 700,000 people assigned to build the Emperor's tomb and terra cotta army, many were serving sentences for stealing and other common crimes. Severe crimes—murder and treason, for example—warranted beheading and other physical mutilation.

Other laborers came from the peasant community already at work in the fields. They resented their transfer to Qin's building projects and the long hours of forced labor there. If they died from overwork, they were quickly replaced by other peasants or lawbreakers. Taking people from their jobs in the fields was risky, though, since agriculture was the source of China's wealth in Qin's time.

Because there were so many laws, some of which were never written down, there was almost constant misunderstanding and ignorance of them. People broke laws without knowing it, particularly laws regarding new standardized weights, measures, and currency. They could barely keep up with the changing rules and regulations under Qin. Many "criminals," therefore, were really uninformed, innocent people, and as history has proved, more talented than anyone imagined.

But Qin accepted no excuses for breaking even the most minor laws. And judging by the stern expressions on the faces of some of his clay soldiers, few deliberately disobeyed him.

A finished soldier stands at the ready.

The stern look on this soldier's face may reflect the harsh policies of Qin's government.

Law and Order

Qin's harsh laws stemmed from the teachings of Han Feizi and from the Emperor's chief advisor, Li Su. They believed in the Legalist doctrine, which warned that a ruler's own staff was his main competition. So to control his ministers, Li Su advised the Emperor to follow Han Feizi's "seven methods":

1. *Know and compare all the various possibilities.*
2. *Punish failure with unvarying severity to the awe in which he is held.*
3. *Grant generous and reliable rewards for success.*
4. *Listen to all views, and hold the proposer responsible for every word.*
5. *Issue unfathomable orders and make deceptive assignments.*
6. *Conceal one's own knowledge when making enquiries of a minister.*
7. *Speak in opposites and act in contraries.*

Though Qin followed the Legalist doctrine and listened to Li Su, he was his own man and made his own rules. He trusted no one completely, yet he rewarded his ministers with promotions, and they promised their loyalty in return. Through them, Qin ruled his people and pursued his goal—to unify China through war and build peace and prosperity through farming. But farming according to Qin's laws was anything but easy. Farmers who failed to distribute grain accurately—as rations for the laborers and salaries for officials—violated the law, and were punished severely. And if grain spoiled because of rain or mouse infestation, those in charge were heavily fined.

"Family morality was also heavily regulated," writes historian Guisso: "A man who repudiated his wife and failed to report it in writing to the authorities was fined two suits of armor. And so was the divorced wife!" A man who discovered his wife had been married before had to divorce her—or endure a long term of forced labor. And his wife received the same sentence. Qin's concept of the role of women reflected the traditional attitude in China; it was "Father knows best" carried to the extreme, and it lasted for centuries.

Qin seemed to have been kinder to animals, as expressed in his code: "Except in the months of summer, one should not venture to burn weeds to make ashes, to collect young animals, eggs or fledglings. One should not . . . poison fish or tortoises or arrange pitfalls or nets. . . . In the season of young animals, one should not venture to take dogs to go hunting."

Qin was especially strict in enforcing standards of excellence in the building of his tomb site, as the Shiji *reports: "Goods had to carry the maker's name, so as to ensure quality, for those who made faulty things were liable to punishment." (After the discovery of the terra cotta army at Mount Li, such markings were found on the bricks forming the floors of the pits.)*

MIRROR OF THE ANCIENT WORLD

Once thought to be legends, the figures from Qin's tomb now offer a link to the past.

Until the discovery of Qin's terra cotta army, we depended on ancient records, songs, and folktales for information about the life and times of China's First Emperor. While his military power was legendary, the strategies of his generals and their powerful offensive capabilities were not well known. And not until the army appeared "live" at Mount Li did we fully appreciate the awesome talent of the ancient Chinese people who spent most of their lives building Qin's tomb and modeling the clay guards who still stand there 2,200 years later.

A face from China's past reflects a view of life centuries old.

As a mirror of the ancient world, the tomb complex reflects both the good and the bad of the First Emperor's reign. In the soldiers' individual facial expressions we see a diverse group of people unified for the first time. We see the birth of China as one country. We see warfare as a way of life and as a way to uncertain peace. We see advanced weaponry never known before in ancient China. We see a fanatic concern with law and order, precision and control. And from the sheer number of soldiers and weapons, we sense more than a love of power; we sense Qin's enormous fear of evil spirits and local rebellion.

As more and more of the tomb site is uncovered, we will learn more about the history of Qin and his people.

Soon after Qin's death in 210 B.C., at the age of 49, the people rebelled against his countless laws and cruel punishments, totally destroyed his empire, and replaced it with a government based on the teachings of Confucius. But the First Emperor left a legacy of achievement unmatched in Chinese history and probably in the world. Only Alexander the Great and Julius Caesar came close. Even today, signs of Qin's accomplishments are everywhere in China—from the roads, canals, currency, and script to the architectural wonders like the Great Wall and the newly discovered terra cotta army. Even Beijing's awesome Forbidden City is but a reflection of the legendary palaces of the First Emperor, as his mysterious tomb may someday reveal.

One of the many treasures created by Qin's craftspeople

A warrior and his horse stand as a monument to the people of China.

While excavation continues at the tomb site near Mount Li, scientists, historians, and tourists stand together by the railing in the Museum of Warrior and Horse Figures and share their impressions of the ancient army standing in formation below. One visitor summed up their reaction. "What strikes me," he said, "is the massive power contained in the statues—and the enormous energy and talent it must have taken to construct them."

Qin's immortality, it turns out, was in the hands of his people all along.

*The Tiananmen Square
demonstration*

Back to the Future

Until the day he died, Qin supervised the construction of his tomb and continued to enlarge his life-size clay army. At the end, he was consumed with fear. Negative thoughts must have plagued him, too. Maybe the people would repudiate his laws someday; maybe they would try to destroy his tomb the way he destroyed the scholars and burned their books; maybe Mencius was right: "Heaven sees accordingly as the people see, Heaven hears accordingly as the people hear." If so, maybe 5,000 soldiers to guard his tomb weren't enough; maybe 7,500 would be better. Always armed and ready: That was the philosophy of Qin Shihuangdi.

More than 2,000 years later, the spirit of the First Emperor—his dark side—seemed to return to the streets of China. In June 1989, while students marched in Beijing's Tiananmen Square to protest the country's authoritarian leadership, the ban on free speech and other human rights, armored tanks moved in to crush the peaceful crowd. Students were killed and their literature burned. And like a giant, dark cloud, the image of Qin's massacre of the scholars seemed to hover over the Square.

Reaction to the Tiananmen tragedy came from all parts of the world. In Minneapolis, Minnesota, Chinese visitors to an exhibition of art from Beijing placed a white floral wreath by the gallery door. A note was attached, and it read: "The blood of the students will nourish the flowers of democracy."

FOR FURTHER READING

Capon, Edmund. *Art and Archaeology in China*. South Melbourne: The Macmillan Company of Australia, 1977.

Cotterell, Arthur. *The First Emperor of China*. London: Penguin Books, 1989.

Guisso, R. W. L., Catherine Pagani, and David Miller. *The First Emperor of China*. New York: Birch Lane Press, 1989.

Qian Hao, Chen Heyi, and Ru Suichu. *Out of China's Earth*. New York: Harry N. Abrams, Inc., 1981.

INDEX

Afang palace 61, 62
agriculture 22, 67
ancestors 24
animals 69
archaeologists 7, 11, 13, 14, 29, 52, 58, 59, 62
armor 25, 34, 35–38, 40, 42, 46, 51, 69
assassination attempts 22

Beijing 21, 74, 77
bronze 44, 49, 50, 52, 54, 62
Burning of the Books 22, 23, 48

Cambridge 14
cavalry 41, 46, 51
China 7, 9, 10, 11, 14, 18, 19, 20, 22, 26, 28, 33, 37, 48, 52, 65, 72, 74, 77
chun-tzu 48
Classic of Music 22
Confucian scholars 22
Confucius 22, 48, 74
Cotterell, Arthur 14, 26, 54, 65

dragon 18

elixir of immortality 26
excavation 14, 44, 57, 60, 62, 75

feudal states 17–18, 48
Five Elements 18
Fu-su, Prince 28

Great Wall 7, 21, 24, 27
Greek sculptors 54
Guisso, R. W. L. 62, 69

Han Feizi 23, 68
huang di 18
Hu-hai 28

immortality 22, 26–28, 61, 75
immortals 26, 28
infantry, infantrymen 33, 34, 36, 40, 41, 51
inscriptions 25

Jacobsen, Robert 7, 13, 14, 29, 30, 58, 59, 63
jade 62
Jia Yi 25

lacquer 35–37, 46
Legalism 22, 69
Li Su 22, 28, 32, 68, 69, 75

Mencius 48, 77
mercury 10, 63
metals 50
mistresses 61
Mount Li 7, 28, 30, 32, 59, 62, 70, 71, 75
Museum of Warrior and Horse Figures 7, 29, 57, 75

palaces 10, 21, 59, 61–64, 74

Qian Hao 50
Qin:
    dynasty 48, 52, 59
    First Emperor 7, 10, 17, 18, 22, 26–27, 52, 63, 74
    tomb of 7, 9, 27, 29, 57, 59, 71

rebellions 22, 48, 72, 74
restoration 57, 58, 60
Ricchiardi, Sherry 31
roads 21, 24, 74

scholars 22, 23, 48, 77
Shaanxi Province 7, 31
Shang Yang 23
"seven methods" 68
Shiji 10, 20, 28, 59, 61, 63, 70
"Sins of Qin, The" 25
symbols 27

Taoism 26
Tiananmen Square 77
"Tiger of China" 18, 19, 28
tomb of the First Emperor 10, 13, 30, 65–67
trees 10, 11, 26

unification of China 9, 20, 22, 69

vegetable dyes 40

warring states 7, 9
Warring States period 19, 37, 54
weapons 14, 25, 29, 46, 48–52,
     62, 72
Wei River 30, 61

Xian 7, 13, 14, 31
Xhou dynasty 18

Yangtze (Yang-tzu) River 10, 26, 62
Yellow River 10, 62
Yellow Sea 28
Ying Zheng 9, 18

Zhou period 54